Beginning Golf

REVISED EDITION

Ben Bruce
Evelyn Davies
Indiana University

D1504385

Wadsworth Publishing Company, Inc.
Belmont, California

L.C. Cat. Card No.: 68-25414

Printed in the United States of America

CONTENTS

1 VALUES   1

2 HISTORY   2

3 EQUIPMENT   4

4 TECHNIQUES OF PARTICIPATION   9

      Description of Grips   10
      Stance, Posture, and Swing   12
      Chipping   19
      Pitching   21
      Hitting from a Hazard   22
      Play from Uneven Terrain   23
      Putting   24
      Strategy   27

5 RULES   32

6 SELF-IMPROVEMENT AND TRAINING   39

7 GLOSSARY   43

8 SELF-TESTING AND EVALUATION   47

9 BIBLIOGRAPHY   56

VALUES

Golf can be as strenuous as you want to make it. Since the golfer sets his own pace, golf can be stimulating or relaxing. Endurance and strength may be improved by increasing the number of holes played and the distance of balls hit. Golf offers the opportunity to be out-of-doors, to walk or ride while enjoying nature and fellowship. It can be challenging, satisfying, and relaxing, even if played during a short period of leisure time. Because it is challenging, golf offers opportunity for sportsmanship, whether alone or with a group.

For those who like competitive games, golf offers a handicap system whereby people of varying abilities may compete in the same tournament or match on an equal basis. This universally accepted system makes allowances for any player's weaknesses in golf.

Golf has become practically a requirement for people interested in the business world. In many business concerns, the fairway has replaced the bridge table, and many business deals are opened or closed on the green. A golf match offers an excellent opportunity to discover some characteristics of your associate, his disposition, self-control, honesty, and ethics. Many business deals have been negated by the "hand mashie," the "foot niblick," or the "memory tally."

Wives have found a way to keep from being golf widows: learn to play the game. Women desirous of staying physically fit and keeping their girlish figures as long as possible have converted daytime bridge clubs into golf groups.

HISTORY

There is no definite date for the origin of golf, but historians credit Holland or the Low Countries with the beginning of a form of golf. Golf seems to have been derived from different activities in which a club or mallet and a ball were used. Pictures indicate a crude type of golf played in other countries long before it became popular in Scotland and England. Counted among the earlier participants were members of English Royalty. James IV was the first to figure formally in the historical record of golf; Mary Stuart was the first woman golfer.

Many golf courses were built before the Royal and Ancient Golf Club of St. Andrews, Scotland, was founded in 1754. St. Andrews, the most famous golf club in the world, is the seat of authority for all matters pertaining to the game. The course has been in constant operation since its inauguration. The established eighteen-hole round was originated with the Royal and Ancient course. The course was laid out with twelve holes. The first eleven ran in a straight line from the clubhouse to the end of a small peninsula. The players played these holes and then returned by playing the first ten greens, plus a green by the clubhouse. Hence the terms "out" on the first half of the course and "in" on the second half were coined. The course consisted of twenty-two holes. When the club decided to make the first four holes only two, the round consisted of eighteen holes (the two eliminated holes had been played twice). Since the Royal and Ancient club set the example, other courses were laid out in eighteen holes.

The first mention of golf in the United States was around 1780, in police records, when "gouff clubs" were noted for play on Sunday. Such play was not in good taste. The first golf courses were built around 1810. Historians usually point to the St. Andrews club near New York City as the first course with a continuous existence. In 1894, five clubs formed an association to govern the game in America. This was the beginning of the *United States Golf Association.*

The game gradually grew in popularity and play. It was considered a game for the wealthy, however, and most play was on private club courses. In 1913, the United States became golf-conscious due to the efforts of a caddy, Francis Ouimet. He won the U.S. Open championship by defeating the two greatest professionals from England, Harry Vardon and Theodore Ray.

In the early part of the twentieth century, women began to show interest in the game, and the pattern was set for golf as we know it today—a game for all. At present about 9,000,000 people play on over 8,000 courses in the United States. International competition is increasing also, as more and more nations pursue the sport.

An interesting parallel with the growth of the game is the constant improvement in the equipment. The first clubs were mere wooden mallets or bats tipped with horn. Balls were made of leather stuffed with enough feathers to fill a hat.

Later, gutta-percha, a gum-like substance, was used in the manufacture of golf balls, and they were round and smooth. Players found that a new ball was very erratic and hard to control; when it was dented and nicked, however, it played much better. When rubber balls were introduced, dimples and dents were incorporated to ensure accuracy in flight. The improvement in ball construction has been so great that the United States Golf Association has set standards of construction to eliminate balls that could impair the challenge and enjoyment of the game.

The introduction of clubs with steel heads and shafts increased the accuracy and consistency of play. Heretofore, shafts were handmade by various artisans to the specifications of the player. The wooden shafts were shaved down for proper whip. Balance was hard to achieve, but with the steel shaft, manufactured under standard conditions, this problem was virtually eliminated. Today shafts are sometimes also made of fiber glass or of aluminum alloy.

EQUIPMENT

3

Golfing equipment consists of clubs, from one to a full set of fourteen, a bag or rack to hold them, balls, and tees.

CLUBS

The beginning golfer may not want a full set of clubs, but he should recognize them and know their uses. Of the fourteen clubs, four may have wooden heads and ten, metal heads. They are designated as woods and irons. The wooden heads are usually made of a polished, high quality wood such as persimmon, while the irons are what their name implies. The shafts of both woods and irons may be hollowed steel, fiber glass, or aluminum alloy, and the grips are usually leather or rubber.

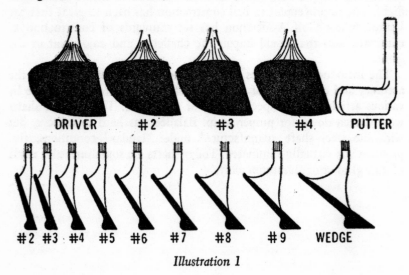

Illustration 1

Today, some wooden club heads are laminated to provide long wear and durability.

The woods are longer than the irons, and the faces of the woods and irons are of different lofts or angles. The higher the number of the club (numbers are found on the sole of the club), the greater the loft of the face. The driver, or number one wood, has a larger head than the other woods; its face is practically vertical. The woods are usually used for longer shots than the irons. The relatively straight face and the long shaft combine to give the ball distance without great height. As the number of the wood increases, so does the loft of the ball, at the expense of distance. The angle of the face largely determines the loft of the ball. The number two wood is very similar to the driver, and golfers frequently substitute this club for the driver on the tee. On the fairway, however, the slight increase in loft of the number two wood enables the golfer to hit the ball from the turf without the added benefit of a tee. Thus the driver is seldom used on the fairway. Where the grass is a bit longer and more loft is needed, a three or four wood may be used.

The irons are numbered in the same manner as the woods: the higher the number, the greater the loft. Thus the two, three, and four irons frequently are used for long shots, the five and six irons for middle distance shots, and the seven, eight, and nine for shots closer to the green. For these close shots, where height, not distance, is needed, the ball should be hit or pitched high in the air, so it will land on the green with little or no roll. The number one iron or driving iron is seldom used by the average golfer and is not included in the standard set. The putter, sometimes referred to as the ten iron, is in a class by itself. Its head is almost perpendicular to the shaft so that the ball can be stroked along the closely mowed grass. The fourteenth club is the wedge, sometimes used to loft the ball from sand, high grass or weeds. This club head is heavier than the others and the face is extremely slanted to ensure the loft of the ball. Selection of the club to be used is an individual matter, and the golfer soon learns which club he needs for each situation.

The selection of clubs becomes one of individual preference, based on length, weight, the "feel" of the club, and the price desired. It is wise to consult a professional at a golf course before purchasing clubs, and to examine some of the many different brands. Since clubs could last for a lifetime, great care should be taken in this initial selection.

Average distances for clubs are as follows (in yards):

CLUB	MEN	WOMEN
1 driver	210–250	150–180
2 wood	200–220	150–170
3 wood	190–210	145–160
4 wood	180–200	140–155
1 iron	180–200	150–180
2 iron	170–190	140–170
3 iron	160–180	130–160
4 iron	150–170	120–150
5 iron	140–160	110–140
6 iron	130–150	100–130
7 iron	120–140	80–120
8 iron	110–130	70–100
9 iron	100–120	60–90
pitching wedge	90–110	50–80
sand wedge	20–40	20–40

BALLS

Golf balls also have a wide price range. Repainted balls or factory rejects are inexpensive and will prove satisfactory for the beginning golfer.

As the golfer's skill improves, the price of his golf balls probably will increase, since the better the ball, the greater the distance possible. Cheaper balls may be satisfactory for the beginner who is prone to lose a few; the thick cover decreases the chances of cutting the ball when the shot is not hit solidly or is topped. Thus the price of golf balls ranges from approximately 35¢ to $1.50.

SHOES

Many students wear canvas shoes for golfing—the same type worn in other activity classes. Street shoes with flat heels may also be worn. High heels are never used. Golf shoes may have thick rubber-rippled soles or spikes to increase the golfer's stability. Spikes may be added to the soles and heels of a pair of Oxfords if the golfer does not want to invest in a pair of golf shoes. Whether spikes or rubber-soled shoes are used, the golfer who maintains balance and stability achieves best results.

TEES, CARTS, AND GLOVES

Tees may be of almost any material, plastic and wood being the most popular and inexpensive. An innovation is a direction arrow attached to the tee to help the golfer stay on course with his swing.

Carts, to be either pulled by hand or driven, may be rented at golf courses. Those that are pulled by hand may be purchased for various prices and may be lightweight or collapsible. Carts may include many accessories to make golfing less strenuous.

A glove is frequently worn on the left hand to ensure a firmer grip and to prevent blisters or calluses. Some gloves cover only the palm; others cover all the fingers. They are usually made of a leather and fabric combination, and come in small, medium, large, and extra large sizes. Most players wear a glove on one hand only; however, gloves may be worn on both hands.

CARE OF EQUIPMENT

Hand-operated ball washers are provided on most tees for cleaning the balls. This little operation saves time when you must hunt for your ball. Clubs should be cleaned after each using, to keep faces and soles free of dirt and grass. If clubs are not cleaned, the grooves in the face will fill, resulting in some loss of spin on the ball. Wipe them with a wet cloth, or wash with mild soap and water. White marks from the ball and other dirt stains may be cleaned by rubbing with a handful of grass. Any good paste wax may be used to keep the woods in good condition and to prevent them from drying or absorbing moisture. Before storing clubs for any length of time, it is advisable to wax them. The storage area should be free from humidity and excess heat to prevent the clubs from warping and rusting. Many people advocate a horizontal position for storing to keep the shafts from bending. To protect the leather grips, it is advisable to rub them lightly with neat's-foot oil a few times a year. The shafts and heads may be kept in good condition by wiping them after each using with a cloth that has a few drops of machine oil on it. If dirt has accumulated on the irons, wash them with mild soap suds, or a mild cleansing agent. Damaged or worn grips, caps, or plugs may be replaced with a do-it-yourself kit, or by any pro shop (professional golfers' shop), for a small fee. Rewinding the club head may also be done at home, but usually better results are achieved by the men in the pro shops. Repairs made by professionals are usually less expensive in the long run.

Head covers, woolen or leather, are used to cover the woods. These protect the woods from being scratched or nicked by banging against the other clubs.

CLOTHING

On the golf course, informal clothing is very popular. As in most public places, however, discretion must be exercised; therefore, short shorts are taboo for women, as is the absence of a shirt for men. Clothes that are comfortable and permit unrestricted movement are preferred; clothing that is too loose or too tight may interfere with the swing and concentration on the shot.

Jewelry, especially rings, may interfere with the grip or swing. Bracelets and watches are not only hazardous and sometimes dangerous, but they are also subject to damage.

GADGETS

There are as many different gadgets and gimmicks as there are swings. Each new gadget is designed to improve the particular swing. Some of these gadgets have helped, or at least the golfer practices more often while trying the gadget, and his golf may improve.

TECHNIQUES
OF PARTICIPATION

4

The objective of golf is to get the ball from the tee into the cup in as few strokes as possible. This presents a challenge to the golfer as he continually tries to lower his score. Competition can be provided by playing an opponent in a variety of ways. Play where the winner is decided on total strokes taken on a specified number of holes is called *stroke play*. The type of play in which the winner is determined by the number of holes won is called *match play*. In match play, the match is ended when a player has won more holes from his opponent than there are holes left to play. For example, when a player has won three more holes than his opponent and there are only two holes remaining to be played, the match ends with the score 3 and 2. Another type of play in which three points are awarded, one for each nine and one for the eighteen holes, whether by stroke or match play, is referred to as *Nassau*.

To enjoy the competition of play one should master the fundamentals of the game. Learning these fundamentals well is essential to a good swing and results in a lower score, the never-ending challenge of golf.

The golf swing cannot be learned in parts. It cannot be taken apart and learned in progression. It is a unified movement, each part dependent upon the others for proper execution; therefore, an understanding of the complete swing is vital. The backswing carries the clubhead back and up in position to start to hit. The downswing brings the clubhead down into the ball with the club face square to the line of flight. The follow-through carries the clubhead through the ball to complete the movement. Although these—the backswing, the downswing, and the follow-through—are discussed separately, they must all be practiced as one complete movement.

The entire body is used in swinging a golf club. The interaction of all parts of the body is transmitted through the hands to the club. The hands, the only connection between body and club, must function properly to ensure consistency in hitting the ball. The grip determines how well the hands operate during the swing. Flaws in body action can result in the hands bringing the clubhead into the ball on the wrong

9

line or with poor timing. These flaws can be corrected, but an improper grip will not yield good results even if all other parts of the swing are perfect. Consistency can be achieved only with a proper grip. Thus the grip is basic in golf.

No two persons' hands and wrists are exactly alike; therefore it would be impossible to describe one grip suitable for all. Three different grips are explained: the *overlapping* or *Vardon*, the *non-lapping*, and the *interlocking*.

DESCRIPTION OF GRIPS

All of these grips are similar and, viewed from the front, their differences are difficult for the inexperienced individual to detect (see Illustration 2). Variations in the grip are achieved mainly by changing

Illustration 2

the position of the little finger of the right hand with respect to the index finger of the left hand.

To acquire the correct grip (for the right-handed person), place the sole of the clubhead on the ground. Let the grip of the club rest diagonally across the forepart of the left hand, from the second joint of the first finger to the heel of the hand. Wrap the fingers around the club with the thumb straight down the shaft or slightly to the right of center. About one inch of the grip should extend beyond the heel of the left hand, to give better balance and freedom of wrist movement than would be obtained by gripping it at the end.

Place the right hand below the left, with the groove of the heel of the palm covering the left thumb. Circle the index finger of the right hand around the club, much as if it were a "trigger finger." The club grip should now rest across the first joint of the index finger and the hand, at the junction of the palm and the other fingers. Close the hand as though you were shaking hands. Place the right thumb along the center of the shaft, or slightly to the left of center, meeting the right forefinger. The grip is firm, but not tight.

VARDON OR OVERLAPPING GRIP

The small finger of the right hand overlaps and grips the knuckle of the left forefinger. Thus, seven fingers contact the club (see Illustration 3).

INTERLOCKING GRIP

The little finger of the right hand interlocks with the first finger of the left hand; thus, six fingers contact the club (see Illustration 4).

NON-LAPPING GRIP

Both hands grip the club, so eight fingers are in contact with the club. This is the strongest and probably the most natural grip for beginners. The hands, although not interlocking or overlapping, should be as close together as possible, enabling the wrists to perform as one unit (see Illustration 5).

In all grips, the club should be held in the fingers, not in the palms. When the palms are pressed against the grip, movement is restricted. This results in "arm hitting," without wrist action, and a loss of power. Also, without the finger grip, the "feel" of the club, or sensitivity to the action of the club, is impaired.

Since no two persons have hands exactly alike, it is impossible to say that any one grip is best for all. One should experiment until he finds the grip that feels best and gives him the best results.

Illustration 3   *Illustration 4*   *Illustration 5*

Checkpoints for Grip

1. If fingernails turn white, the club is being gripped too tightly.

2. The V's formed by the thumb and forefinger of each hand point somewhere between the chin and right ear.

3. When looking at the hands, see *no more than* two knuckles of each hand. Don't peek!

4. The thumb of the left hand rests slightly to the right of the midline of the shaft.

5. The thumb of the right hand rests slightly to the left of center of the shaft, meeting the forefinger.

6. The club is held primarily by the fingers, the last three of the left hand and the middle two of the right hand are the key to a good grip.

7. The hands are as close together as possible, acting as one unit.

STANCE, POSTURE, AND SWING

Golf is an individual activity. The golf swing is influenced by the individual's build and his rhythm of movement. For instance, a tall, slender person may have a longer swing than a short, stocky person, whose swing may be more compact. This may not always be true, but it is one example of the effect that different body types have on golf swings. The relationship of body parts changes with the execution of the swing, and the smoothness of this swing is dependent upon the individual's movement patterns.

There are a few principles that must be followed to hit the ball consistently. These principles are concerned with stability achieved by the body being well-balanced over the feet. Stability and balance of all body parts must be maintained even when the rotation of the body results in the weight being shifted from one foot to the other.

Though the position of the feet may change in addressing the ball, depending on the lie of the ball and the club used, the weight must be balanced over the feet to ensure a well-hit shot. A ball hit from a balanced position requires less effort than a ball hit when the player is off balance.

STANCE

Three positions assumed when hitting the ball are: *square stance, open stance,* and *closed stance.* These terms describe the placement of the feet in relation to the intended line of flight. In each stance the toes point outward slightly.

Square Stance. The square stance is achieved by placing the feet in a line parallel with the desired flight of the ball (see Illustration 6). This basic stance could suffice for all shots for a beginner.

Closed Stance. The closed stance finds the left foot closer to the direction or flight line than the right foot (see Illustration 6).

Open Stance. The right foot is closer to the line of direction than the left foot, and the body is turned slightly toward the hole (see Illustration 6).

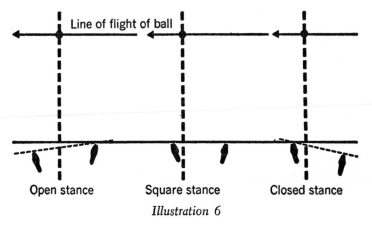

Illustration 6

The foot position chosen depends upon the club used, the type of swing needed, and the desired flight of the ball. It is well to note that the tee markers are not necessarily direction indicators and should not be relied upon for lining up your shot.

Stance Related to Club

Usually the closed stance is used when driving from the tee or hitting a long fairway shot. This stance permits a full swing and results in greater distance. Placing the feet a bit farther apart than shoulder width and using the closed stance makes it possible to maintain balance while the hips and shoulders rotate and the arms swing freely from the shoulders. Thus a fluid movement is produced.

Golfers tend to employ the square stance for the middle distance iron shots, i.e. four, five, and six irons.

When the shorter irons are used, the open stance is taken to accommodate a shorter backswing for a more controlled hit. Use of the open stance enables the golfer to keep his arms closer to his body and to decrease rotation of his hips.

Stance and Posture

Regardless of the stance taken, the sole of the club is placed on the ground directly behind the ball. The hands assume the preferred grip, with the right elbow bent slightly, the left arm extended. Both elbows point toward the pockets. Although the waist is bent slightly, a straight line is maintained from the hips to the head. (It is extremely difficult to hit a golf ball from a crouched position.) The result should be a comfortable stance at the right distance from the ball to enable one to hit with force and control.

Posture and Swing

To ensure a smooth, even swing or a rhythmical, synchronized swing, it is imperative that a stable base be maintained throughout. Place the feet a comfortable distance apart with the weight pulled toward the inside of the ankles, slightly forward on the balls of the feet. This position is not to be exaggerated, but it should give a feeling of firmness with the ground.

Flex the knees slightly to give a comfortable and relaxed feeling. This will also put the weight on the balls of the feet.

Bend the trunk forward, as explained above, and hold the head stationary with the eyes focused on the ball.

Let the arms hang comfortably from the shoulders. The right arm will extend a bit below the left, because the right hand is placed below the left hand on the grip.

With a proper stance—the weight balanced over the feet, knees relaxed, trunk bent forward at the waist, head down, eyes focused on the ball—and the correct grip, the golfer is ready to hit the ball.

Illustration 7

Many golfers find that a preliminary waggle (lifting the club and replacing it while addressing the ball) helps to release tension, aids in securing a better footing, helps in seeing that the clubhead is in correct position, and aids in reminding them to use their wrists. The swing should be started from a feeling of motion, rather than from a static position—thus the waggle.

BACKSWING

The only function of the backswing is to get the club into position to hit the ball. If the club is brought back correctly, it is in position to contact the ball. In other words, the downswing of the club should approximate the path of the backswing (see Illus. 8).

To bring the club back correctly, guide the club with the arms and shoulders along a straight line from the ball until the hands are in front

Illustration 8

of the right knee. Due to rotation of shoulders and hips the weight slowly shifts to the right leg, allowing the left knee to move in and slightly down in a direction behind the ball. This causes the left heel to raise a few inches from the ground. The right leg, with the knee relaxed, maintains a straight balanced position. The arms continue in an upward arc, until the left shoulder is under the chin. The right elbow should point toward the ground throughout the backswing. At the top of the backswing, the club should not drop below a line parallel with the ground. If it does, the club will have to be lifted to start the downswing, resulting in wasted motion and loss of awareness of the clubhead. In golf, the application of force should be down (Illus. 9)!

At the top of the arc, the weight should be on the right leg with the left arm as straight as possible. At this point, start to uncoil the body. This action causes the weight to shift to the left leg. Let the arms bring the clubhead down through the same arc it followed on the backswing. This entire action is initiated by the left side of the body (Illus. 10).

Illustration 9   *Illustration 10*

DOWNSWING AND CONTACT

At the point of contact with the ball, the wrists are firm, allowing the whole unbroken impact of the body's uncoiling to be transmitted through the clubhead to the ball. As the weight is being transferred to the left leg, the left knee is relaxed; but as was stated previously, a stable base is maintained, around which the hips and shoulders rotate. Since the force is *through* and not *at* the ball, the clubhead follows the path of the ball until the arms are fully extended. For hitting shots with an iron, emphasize the downward force. As the face of the club descends on the ball, it continues downward into the turf. The ball is contacted before the turf. As the club face meets the ball and continues downward after contact it imparts a reverse or backspin to the ball. This spinning action has an effect of lifting the ball in flight and retarding forward roll when the ball lands. To achieve this action a little turf must be taken on all iron shots.

FOLLOW-THROUGH

Momentum carries the clubhead through the rest of the arc, bringing it up over the left shoulder. Let the clubhead follow the flight of the ball as long as possible. At the end of the follow-through, the right shoulder is under the chin, and the body weight is over the left foot, more toward the toes than toward the heel. This causes the head to be raised to watch the flight of the ball.

The head is an anchor point, or the hub of an arc, around which the arms swing. The arms are the radius of the arc. Thus the head remains stationary; on the backswing the left arm remains straight; both arms straighten on the downswing when force is applied and contact is made; and the arc is maintained on the follow-through by the straight right arm acting as the radius of the arc (see Illus. 11).

In a smoothly executed swing, there is fluid movement from the waggle right on through the backswing, downswing and follow-through.

Illustration 11

Checkpoints for Stance, Posture, and Swing

1. Toes should be outward, knees slightly flexed, trunk forward, back straight, and head stationary.

2. Weight must be balanced for the specific shot.

3. At address, the left hand should hide the left kneecap.

4. As the hands pass the right leg, the club shaft is parallel to the ground with the toe of the club pointing up.

5. When hands are slightly past the right leg, the wrists begin to flex.

6. At the top of the backswing, the club does not go beyond a line parallel with the ground.

7. The wrist should remain cocked until just prior to contact with the ball.

8. Force should always be down!

9. Don't hit at the ball—let the club meet the ball during the natural swing.

These checkpoints are basic principles related to stance, posture, and swing for all golf strokes taken with a full swing. However, there are circumstances that require an altering of the swing. The nearness to the green, the lie of the ball, and hazards are examples. In these cases a player may alter his stance, posture, or swing to meet the demands of the stroke. These shots are explained in detail under the specific headings of Chipping, Pitching, Hitting from a Hazard, Play from Uneven Terrain, and Putting.

CHIPPING

Beginning golfers frequently fail to recognize the importance of a well-executed chip shot; they waste many valuable strokes by hitting the ball back and forth across the green. The chip shot is used when the ball rests a few feet from the green, usually 3–15 feet, too far to putt and too short to pitch. The chip is made with a four, five, six, or seven iron. The choice of club depends on distance, type of grass from which

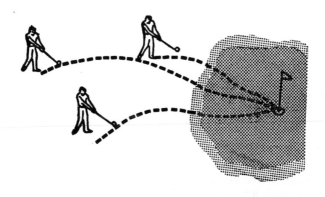

Illustration 12

the ball is hit, slope of the green, and the amount of green between the ball and the pin. A general rule is that the closer the ball is to the green, the lower the number of club used. If the ball is in deep grass, the higher-numbered club is used, and a firm stroke is taken. Go down after the ball! If the green slopes away, the ball will have more roll, so a higher-numbered club is used to decrease the roll. Hitting uphill requires more force than usual, since the ball will have less roll. If there is considerable distance from the edge of the green and the flagstick, a lower-numbered club should be used.

Make the chip shot with feet close together and knees bent slightly, as though you were starting to sit. Most of the action is performed by the arms. Bend wrist sharply on the backswing of the chip shot. The length of the backswing determines the force with which the ball will be hit. Bring the club down into the ball and carry it through, low to the ground and in line with the flight of the ball. This is not a chopping motion; it is more a sweeping motion. The left wrist is firm at impact, moving the club low along the grass. "Picking" the ball may cause a poor shot, or may impart backspin, which would stop the roll of the ball.

Keep the ball low and hit it to a predetermined spot on the green from where it should roll or "run" to the cup. The object of the chip shot is to secure enough loft to lift it over the fringe or apron of the green, and place it close enough to hole out on the next stroke (see Illus. 12).

Checkpoints for Chipping

1. Stand with feet close together.
2. Bend knees slightly, as though starting to sit.
3. Play ball off left heel.
4. Left wrist should be firm at contact.
5. Follow through along path of ball.
6. Use wrists and arms mainly.
7. Never let the club head pass the left hand.
8. Keep flight of ball low.
9. Hit to a predetermined spot and have ball roll to the cup, near enough for an easy one putt.

PITCHING

The pitch shot is used when the ball is from 15 feet to 75 yards from the green. The eight or nine iron or a pitching wedge is used to give the ball loft and backspin. This shot is hit high to a spot near the flagstick, where backspin causes it to stop. Assume the stance with the feet 10–15 inches apart, and flex the knees slightly more than for a regular iron shot. The hand and wrist action is vital to this shot, but little body action is needed. Play the ball off a line from the inside of the left heel.

Lift the club rather sharply on the backswing, to bring the clubhead in position to hit down and through the ball. The clubhead should follow a line toward the cup on the follow-through. Too much body movement causes the shot to be pulled. The angle of the club face determines the loft; the action of the clubhead gives the ball a reverse spin to make it stop. Do not attempt to lift the ball by swinging up on the follow-through, or to impart backspin by chopping down on the downswing (see Illus. 13).

Generally the length of the backswing determines the distance of the shot. Whether the shot is 75 yards or 15 feet, the wrist and hand action is the same. The length of the backswing determines the head speed, which is responsible for the distance, and the snap of the wrist causes backspin. Thus, the same shot is used regardless of distance desired. Both backswing and follow-through should be short and crisp. If the

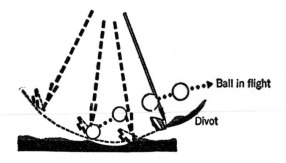

Ball in flight

Divot

Illustration 13

club is brought back to a full backswing and eased into the ball, the turf is usually hit first, resulting in a soft shot with little backspin.

Checkpoints for Pitching

1. Stand with feet 10–15 inches apart.
2. Lift club sharply on backswing.
3. Make backswing and follow-through short and crisp.
4. Contact ball before turf.
5. Hit down and through the ball.

HITTING FROM A HAZARD

The bunker or sand trap shot is probably the most feared in golf. If a bunker shot is played properly, there is little to fear. Most golfers see the pros blast out of a bunker and think every bunker shot should be blasted. Hit the ball firmly at all times, but blast only when the ball is imbedded in the sand so deeply that it must be dug out with the shot.

The bunker shot is made from an open stance, and, like all other shots, must be made with a firm base. While assuming the stance, wiggle the feet around until they are settled firmly in the sand. Since

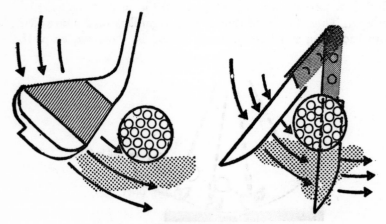

Illustration 14

the club may not touch the sand before the downswing, wiggling the feet into position affords opportunity for testing the sand's consistency.

Aim at a point immediately behind the ball. If the aim is directly at the ball, there is a tendency to top the ball. The club face should be slightly open or laid back as the backswing is started. Cock the wrist more sharply than on the full swing, since the club must be lifted rather than drawn back along the surface of the hazard. To lift the ball from the hazard, it is vital that the stroke be *down* into the sand at the point of aim. The club should enter the sand much like a knife cutting under the ball. Take only as much sand as is necessary to hit the ball firmly. When contact is made with the ball, the club continues to follow through the sand. Don't punch the shot. Always follow through. If the ball is picked too cleanly, it will sail over the green; if the club digs too deeply, the ball will move very little.

Checkpoints for Hitting from a Hazard

1. Use an open stance.
2. Wiggle the feet into the sand to secure a firm base.
3. Aim just far enough behind the ball to ensure a firm hit.
4. Always follow through.
5. Make the club meet the sand like a knife slicing under the ball (see Illus. 14).

PLAY FROM UNEVEN TERRAIN

Surfaces in actual play will not be as level as the practice tees. A player must know what to expect from a shot hit from an uphill, downhill, or sidehill lie. Generally, a ball hit from an uphill lie, or a lie in which the ball is higher than the feet, is hooked or pulled; that is, the ball travels to the left of the intended line of flight, partly because of the delay of the weight shift to the left foot. A ball hit from a downhill lie, or a lie in which the ball is lower than the feet, is sliced or pushed (travels to the right) because the tendency is to shift the weight to the left foot too soon. In both instances, the lowest part of the swing arc is not exactly in the middle of the swing.

In playing an uphill lie, a longer club, usually one or two numbers lower than the club normally selected, is used to compensate for the added loft to the ball, because of hitting along the contour of the terrain on the follow-through. On a downhill lie, a more lofted club is used to hit the ball into the air. The ball should be played opposite the foot that is on higher ground, i.e., left for uphill, right for downhill. For each shot, the backswing and follow-through follow the contour of the ground, and extra effort is made to get the proper shift of weight during the swing. Always take a practice swing before attempting a shot, to get the feel of the terrain.

When the ball is higher than the feet, move the hands down the grip to equalize the height of the ball in relation to the feet. Use the club normally used for the shot; little distance loss will occur. With this lie, it would be wise to allow for some hook or pull rather than to try to change the swing to get a straight ball. Should the ball be lower than the feet, stand closer. The swing will be more upright than usual and the force of the swing will tend to pull the body forward. Most of the weight rests on the heels to resist this forward pull. With this lie, make allowances for a slight slice or fade to the right.

Checkpoints for Play on Uneven Terrain

1. Play ball opposite uphill foot.
2. Increase club length for uphill lies; decrease for downhill.
3. Follow contour of hill with backswing and follow-through.
4. Shorten grip when ball is above feet.
5. Stand closer to ball when ball is below feet.

PUTTING

Putting, one of the most important parts of golf, is the most neglected by many golfers. Par for an eighteen-hole round, on most courses, allows for thirty-six putts—or at least half the total strokes. Thus, putting affords an opportunity to shave strokes from the score. A short putt counts as much as a booming drive, but hurts more when missed. Many of the best golfers are excellent putters, and when they hit a slump in other parts of their games, they make up the difference on the greens.

Illustration 15

Putting is an entirely different department of golf. The object is to roll the ball into the cup with a sure, smooth stroke. There are almost as many different putting forms as there are golfers, but these forms all follow a few basic fundamentals. In general, the stance is such that it restricts body movement, the eyes are directly over the ball, the grip is a light one, and the stroke is made *through* the ball. Stances vary so greatly that it would be foolish to say that any one stance is superior to another. The majority of the touring professionals putt from a slightly open stance, play the ball off the left toe, and rest the weight on the left foot. The head is kept directly over the ball and the right elbow held fairly close to the body. This inhibits body movement in the stroke (see Illus. 15).

The reverse overlap grip is used the most in putting. The first finger of the left hand overlaps the little finger of the right hand, allowing for more feel of the stroke with the right hand. The first three fingers of the right hand hold the club firmly, while the left hand stabilizes the club (see Illus. 16).

Putting calls for much mental effort as well as physical skill. A player must be able to read a green, feel a shot, have confidence, and be relaxed and able to concentrate. Confidence and feel go hand in hand, for if one is able to feel sure of the hit and see the ball start on its way,

Illustration 16

he knows it is going into the cup. Some days the feel or touch may be lost, while on others the ability to concentrate may be lacking. On these days, the score may reveal a disheartening total.

To read the green is to judge how much slope or roll there is on the green, so the ball can be hit on a line or in an arc that will carry it to the cup. Other factors that enter into reading the green are: the nap or grain, the speed, the amount of moisture or dew, and the degree and direction of the roll of the green.

After reading the green and deciding on the line or arc to be followed, address the ball and think the putt through. The ball must be hit hard enough for it to drop into the cup. Hitting the ball too easy is as poor a shot as hitting it too hard—they both require additional strokes to hole out.

Bring the club back with the wrists and forearms. The clubhead is kept low and square to the line of putt. Then swing the club forward through the ball, still on a straight line. This stroke causes the ball to roll smoothly on the green. If the club is lifted after hitting the ball, the ball will hop and go off line.

On short putts, tap or pop the ball into the cup. Bring the club back a short distance, then take it through to hit the ball with a firm tapping movement. There is little follow-through, and the feeling is as though you were hitting a tack with a hammer.

A word of caution: avoid "overstudying" a putt, and don't address the ball for a lengthy period. These actions create tension and usually result in a poor shot. If you feel yourself becoming tense, step back and take a practice swing to relax.

Checkpoints for Putting

1. Use a stance that is comfortable but limits body movement.
2. Do not move shoulders—putting is a wrist and arm stroke.
3. Hold head directly over the ball.
4. Hold club lightly but firmly.
5. Keep club face square to the line of the putt.
6. Rest putter softly behind the ball at the beginning of the stroke. Do not press down on the green at the address.
7. Bring club back smoothly and keep it low, close to the green.
8. Follow through with a smooth, forward sweeping movement, keeping clubhead on the line of the putt.
9. Keep hands even with the ball on impact.

STRATEGY

Plan your play. Playing any round of golf calls for intelligent thinking and planning to achieve the best results. A player who uses good judgment will score better than one who shoots with reckless abandon and with little concern for strategy.

1. *Avoid tension.* Many times when a golfer is playing before a group, tension can cause a poor shot. Always take practice swings to ensure a good stroke. Blot out the spectators from your mind. Hit the ball as though it were a practice shot. Frequently, overstudying a putt causes tension and thus stroking off line. If tension is felt at the address, walk away from the ball and relax.

2. *Take the offensive.* Hit all shots so they will force your opponents to try to do as well or better. Don't be concerned if an opponent hits a longer drive than you do. You have the opportunity to hit the green in position for a par or birdie, while the burden of getting as close as your ball rests with your opponent. Play the course, and induce your opponent to play your game.

3. *Allow for mistakes.* A match is no place to experiment with your game. If you are slicing, play to the left side so that the ball will come to rest in the middle of the fairway. If you are pulling your pitch shots consistently, aim for the right side of the green. If the error is a minor one, make the correction, but don't experiment; you may lose the match.

4. *Don't gamble.* When the opponent has the advantage, too many players attempt shots of which they are incapable. For example, an opponent may be on the green in two strokes, 20 feet from the flagstick, while you may be in the bunker in the same number of strokes, with the flagstick quite near the edge of the bunker. If you try to play the ball close to the pin rather than merely to the green, you may find the next shot still in the sand. Trying to hit the flagstick every time is too risky and may add extra strokes. All long approach shots should be played to the center of the green; short pitch or chip shots may be aimed at the flagstick without as much chance for error.

When in the deep rough, don't try for distance, but play for position on the next shot. Be more concerned with getting a decent shot from the rough than with attempting to hit the green (see Illus. 17).

5. *Concentrate.* Play each shot as it comes. Attempting to figure too far ahead may cause a poor shot. Think each stroke through, visualize the ball in flight, think positively. If you are convinced you can't hit a shot, or sure it will slice or hook, in all probability it will. Decide how the shot should be played, then play it that way. If on your backswing you feel you have too much club, trying to compensate with an easy swing will probably result in a poor and inaccurate shot. A poor shot should be forgotten and not allowed to influence the next stroke. Be careful in selection of club.

6. *Play in turn.* When near or on the green, many players think they are being courteous by hitting their ball as soon as they come to it, instead of waiting for the person who is away. The player having the right to hit first should be allowed to do so. Hitting out of turn may cause a poor shot, and thus encourage the opponent, or place him in a position to play safe on his shot.

7. *Lag or "lay-up" on putts.* The objective of a putt is to get the ball into the cup. There are times, however, when it is wise to play just close enough to assure sinking the next shot. An example of this strategy may be found in the following situation: the opponent is 30 feet from the flagstick in three strokes, and you are 45 feet from the flagstick in two strokes. You need only two putts for a tie, if he sinks his next shot. You may be sure of a tie and a possible win if you don't three-putt. In this situation, it would be better to lag to within a foot or so from the cup, rather than to try to sink the putt, only to roll the ball several feet beyond and three-putt.

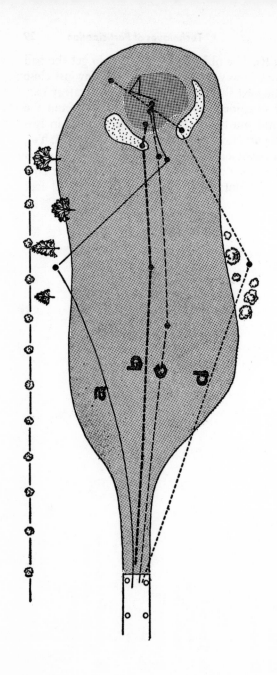

Illustration 17

STRATEGY	RESULT	DISADVANTAGE	ADVANTAGE
First Shot			
A. Attempts to drive green	Over-swings	Loss of control	None
B. Plays cautiously	Well-placed drive	None	In good position for approach
C. Plays overcautiously	Short drive	Long approach shot	None
D. Attempts to excel B	Pushed shot	Difficult lie in rough with poor approach	None
Second Shot			
A. Does not attempt to hit over tree and avoids bunker (plays safe)	Well-placed approach	None	Easy chip shot to pin
B. Attempts to hit to pin	Lands in bunker	Difficult recovery	None
C. Plays to middle of green but erred in judgment in club selection	Short of green	Has chip shot remaining	None
D. Attempts to play over bunker, rather than playing safe	Lands in bunker	Difficult lie	None

RULES

5

Golf is a social game; thus observance of rules of the game and behavior on the course is important for enjoyable play. To disregard these elements of the game is to alienate oneself from other players.

Etiquette governing play is presented on the next few pages, followed by the more important and commonly used rules. In a book of this type, it would be impractical to list all the rules, but a Rule Book may be purchased from the United States Golf Association, 40 East 38th Street, New York 16, New York. For interpretation of specific rules, see a golf professional.

PROCEDURE FOR STARTING PLAY

Before playing golf—alone, with a partner, or in a foursome—you must report to the starter. He is usually in or near the pro shop, where players register, pay fees, and receive starting times or numbers. If there is little play on the course, you will be told to go right out, or to follow the foursome on the tee.

If the course is a popular one, players must wait their turns. Frequently, when waiting for their numbers to be called over the loudspeaker, golfers use the practice green to improve their putting. Individual players and twosomes are often requested to join others to complete foursomes. This is done to expedite play, since a foursome takes precedence over a single player, a twosome, or a threesome.

In many places, starting times on weekends must be reserved a week ahead. Other courses will not take reservations and golfers must stand in line awaiting tee times.

On those courses where the amount of play does not warrant pre-arranged starting times nor highly organized systems of starting, simpler methods may be used. Among these is one whereby one member of a playing group tees his ball outside the teeing ground. One player from each following group tees his ball behind the first in order of arrival. The starting order has thus been established. The player whose ball is at the head of the line removes it and moves to the teeing ground. A similar procedure is followed when a ball rack or tube is provided. Each member drops a ball in the top of the rack or tube on arrival. The member whose ball drops to the bottom of the rack or tube removes it and goes to the teeing ground.

ETIQUETTE DURING PLAY

1. To prevent distraction, do not talk, move, or stand close to or directly behind the ball, the player, or the hole, when a stroke is being made.

2. Always play without undue delay.

3. Do not attempt a stroke as long as the players in front are within range.

4. The player with the honor plays first. (For a definition of *honor*, see Glossary.) The player who is away continues to hit until his ball rests nearer the flagstick than another player's.

5. Rake all holes and footprints made in a bunker.

6. When searching for a lost ball, allow players following to pass; signal them to pass, and do not continue play until they are out of range.

7. Each player is responsible for replacing and pressing down any turf cut or displaced by him. Repair any damage made to the green. (A tee can be used to level ball marks made on the green.)

8. Every precaution should be taken to prevent damage to the green. Do not drop the flagstick, stand close to the cup, drop or lay bags on the green, pull carts across the green, drag shoe spikes across the green, or replace the flagstick improperly.

9. Do not delay on the green. Scores should be tallied after leaving the putting green. Do not practice on the green.

10. Exercise caution against walking in the line of another player's putt, or casting a shadow across the hole or across the line of putt when another player is addressing his ball.

11. A warning shout of "Fore" is given when a ball is hit in the direction of or close to other players. When you hear "Fore," don't turn to face the ball, and don't run. Either of these actions may cause you to move into the path of the ball. The proper action is to bend over, facing away from the warning, and to cover the head with the arms.

12. The most general rule in golf is: *Be courteous!*

FORMAL RULES

The rules of golf are the same the world over, and the ruling body is the Royal and Ancient Golf Club of St. Andrews, Scotland. The United States and Canada are the only two nations who have their own ruling organization, the United States Golf Association. This association, in agreement with the Royal and Ancient Golf Club of St. Andrews, modifies rules concerning play and equipment in the United States and Canada. Rule differences between these two organizations are usually very slight. The Professional Golfers Association, or PGA, is an organization of professional golfers. This organization does not formulate the rules for play and should not be confused with the ruling body, the United States Golf Association.

The rules of golf are numerous and, in many cases, complex. Many golfers are unaware that they are violating some of the less common rules when they ask advice, sole the club in a hazard, or play the wrong ball. For purposes of expediency, the rules are explained in a general way. These rules are subject to change, so a check with a professional or a copy of the United States Golf Association Rule Book is advisable.

RULES PERTAINING TO THE TEEING AREA

1. All clubs used shall conform to United States Golf Association specifications, and no more than fourteen clubs shall be used. A player may replace a club that has broken during play. Most manufacturers make their clubs in conformance with United States Golf Association specifications. The penalty for carrying more than fourteen clubs is two strokes per club for the hole on which the rule was violated in stroke play, and loss of hole in match play. However, the penalty may not exceed four strokes or the loss of two holes regardless of when the violation is discovered.

2. When starting play on a hole, the ball must be teed within the teeing area—that area two club lengths in depth, the front and sides of which are defined by the outside limits of two tee markers. For violation in match play, the opponent may require the player to replay the ball within the teeing ground with no penalty. In stroke play, the stroke taken outside the teeing ground is counted as well as any other stroke so made, and then the player must play within the teeing ground, with the right of teeing his ball.

3. Should a ball fall off the tee, or be knocked off accidentally during the address, it shall be re-teed without penalty.

RULES FROM TEE TO GREEN

1. *Ball lost or out-of-bounds.* A ball is to be treated as lost or out-of-bounds after reasonable evidence to this effect is shown or a search of five minutes has been made. An honest attempt must be made to find the ball. Penalty: loss of distance and one penalty stroke. The player must play his next stroke as near as possible to the spot from which the original ball was played.

2. *Provisional ball.* If there is doubt as to whether a ball is lost or out-of-bounds, the player may play another from as near as possible to the spot where the original ball was played. This is done to save time and avoid going back after the ball is declared lost. The player must announce his intention of playing a provisional ball. He may play the provisional ball until he reaches the place where the original ball is likely to be. If the original ball is lost or out of bounds, he shall incur the penalty and continue play with the provisional ball.

3. *Ball unplayable.* The player is the only one who may declare the ball unplayable. If the ball is so declared, the player has three options: (1) Drop a ball two club lengths from where the original ball rests, but no nearer the hole, under penalty of one stroke; (2) drop a ball as near as possible to the spot from where the original ball was played, adding one stroke; or (3) drop a ball behind the unplayable spot keeping that spot in line with the flagstick and his ball, adding one stroke. Options (1) and (3) result in loss of stroke only; option (2) in loss of stroke and distance. The player should always choose the option that will give him the advantage.

4. *Dropping a ball.* To drop a ball, the player faces the hole and drops the ball over his shoulder, while standing erect. Any other method of dropping the ball shall result in a penalty. The ball should be dropped as near as possible to the original spot, even when in a hazard. Should a ball be dropped and roll into a hazard, it may be dropped again.

5. *Improvement of lie.* Nothing may be done to improve the lie of the ball in the rough or long grass. A ball may not be lifted, and only as much of the long grass may be moved as is necessary to identify the ball. Impediments such as dead leaves and twigs may be removed, as long as the ball is not moved in the process.

6. *Hitting wrong ball.* A player is responsible for the identification of his own ball. This identification includes the brand name and number. Should he play the wrong ball in stroke play, the penalty is two strokes; then he must play his own ball. In match play, he loses the hole. Any strokes made while playing the wrong ball do not count in the score.

7. *Ball unfit for play.* Should a ball become damaged to the extent that it is unfit for play, then and only then may it be replaced without penalty. Should a ball that is not unfit be replaced, a penalty of two strokes in stroke play and loss of hole in match play shall be inflicted.

8. *Playing from hazards.* A player may not touch his club to the sand or water before taking his stroke, under penalty of two strokes in stroke play and loss of hole in match play.

RULES ON THE GREEN

1. *Cleaning ball.* A ball on the putting green may be lifted only once without penalty to be cleaned, and must be replaced on the spot from which it was lifted.

2. *Improving putting surface.* Nothing may be done to improve the surface of the putting green, except to brush away any loose impediment from the line of putt, under penalty of two strokes or loss of hole.

3. *Moving ball on green.* Should a ball rest on the intended line of putt, request may be made for its removal, with the spot marked.

4. *Hitting ball against flagstick.* A player may at any time have the flagstick attended, removed, or held up to indicate the position of the hole. Should the flagstick be removed, it should be carried to the apron of the green, so that it will not interfere with play. If the flagstick is attended, or removed, and the player does not object, he is deemed to have authorized it. Should a ball hit a flagstick while attended, or should it hit the person holding the flagstick, a penalty of two strokes in stroke play and loss of hole in match play shall be given. If a ball on the putting surface hits an unattended flagstick, it shall result in a two-stroke penalty or loss of hole.

GENERAL RULES

1. *Receiving or giving advice.* It is illegal to ask for or receive advice from anyone except your caddy, your partner, or his caddy. The penalty is two strokes or loss of hole.

2. *Checking score.* Each player is responsible for the correctness of his score on any hole, at the conclusion of the round. Should a score be recorded that is higher than the actual number of strokes taken, it shall remain as recorded. If the score is recorded as lower than the actual number of strokes taken, the player shall be disqualified.

3. *Playing on ground under repair.* On occasions, areas of the course may be under repair. These areas are usually marked "Ground under repair," and should not be considered hazards. The privilege of dropping a ball without penalty is allowed.

4. *Designating use of specific club.* No rule designates clubs for particular shots. For example, a sand wedge need not be used in a bunker, nor a driver off the tee.

5. *Lifting ball from non-hazards.* Standing water and holes of burrowing animals or reptiles are not hazards, and a player may lift and drop a ball as near as possible to the spot where it lay (but not nearer the hole) without penalty.

6. *Playing near fixed or immovable obstructions.* Buildings, water hydrants and other similar immovable obstructions are not hazards. Should these interfere with the swing or stance, the ball may be lifted and dropped, within two club lengths from the obstruction (no nearer the hole) without penalty.

SUMMARY OF PENALTIES FOR RULE INFRACTIONS

Loss of Distance *and one stroke*	*Match Play* Loss of hole	*Stroke Play* Two strokes	*One stroke*
1. Out of bounds 2. Lost ball 3. Unplayable lie 4. Water hazard	1. Having more than 14 clubs (Max.—4 strokes or loss of 2 holes) 2. Moving ball at address. (Except on teeing ground) 3. Improving lie. 4. Playing wrong ball. 5. Touching hazard at address or on backswing. 6. Hitting an attended flagstick. 7. Hitting an unattended flagstick from play on the putting surface. 8. Improving line of putt. 9. Playing a practice stroke during play.		1. Unplayable lie 2. Water hazard

SELF-IMPROVEMENT AND TRAINING

PRACTICE

Golf is an individual sport and does not lend itself well to group or team practice. It would be as useless, however, for a player to practice with no plan in mind as it would for a coach to direct practice with no drills or plan of action.

Before undertaking any practice sessions, ask yourself, "What do I need to practice most? How can I best overcome these weak spots in my game? With these questions in mind, plan a course of action. If, for example, drives have been erratic and some work needs to be done on the tee shot, it would be a waste of time to hit ball after ball with no effort to discover the cause of the trouble. A few brief suggestions about practice on different parts of the game may be helpful.

WOODS

Warm up before hitting practice shots, either from a tee or from the turf. Swinging two clubs at one time or swinging a club with a weighted head cover may help to overcome stiffness. Swinging the driver naturally, without attempting to hit the ball, enables you to check the rhythm of the swing. Swinging the club to a waltz tune also can be helpful in improving the rhythm.

Check the grip to be sure the club is held properly. (Most professionals agree that much of the difficulty with woods is traced to the hands.)

Accuracy is more important than distance and you should constantly strive for accuracy in practice as well as in actual play.

Always hit toward a target. A tree in the distance, a stake placed in the ground, or any kind of marker will do, as long as it is a target. If the ball constantly goes to one side, check the stance and body alignment. To check the path of the clubhead, place one tee about 10–12 inches behind the ball and another at the same distance in front of the ball.

As the club is brought back, the tee behind the ball should be knocked over, while the front tee should be loosened on the follow-through. If the swing is from the outside in (causing a slice), or from the inside out (causing a hook), one or both tees will not be hit.

One method of assuring that the left arm is not bent on the backswing is to cut out both ends of a milk carton and slip it over the left elbow. Any strain on the milk carton felt in the elbow will indicate some bending. Do not try to hit with the carton on the arm, because it will restrict bending the arm on the follow-through and result in an unnatural and uncomfortable feeling. Practice only the backswing and the downswing with the carton.

IRONS

Hit iron shots to a target at a specific distance. If, for instance, the distance for a five iron shot is about 150 yards, hit with that iron toward a target 150 yards away. This also will aid in judging distances. Hitting iron shots from a tee may prove harmful when you face the actual playing situation of hitting from the turf. Take turf on all iron shots. It is better to hit into the ground a few times in practice than to miss a shot in play where each stroke counts.

Chipping and Pitching

When practicing the chip and pitch shots, always hit to a target, preferably a practice green. If no green is available, a long section of rope or string laid in a circle is a good target. Use this as an imaginary green and hit to it, making all shots land inside the area. If pitch shots are constantly being pulled to the left, check for too much rotation of the hips and shoulders. If the shots are pushed to the right, check the follow-through to make sure the clubhead is following the intended line of flight to the pin. Remember, on a pitch shot, the club hits *through*, not *to*, the ball.

Putting

Far too few players practice putting as diligently as they should. For a warm-up to putting, hit a few balls to feel the stroke. These shots need not be to a cup, since they are only to get the feel of the club and the smoothness of the stroke. When putting to a cup, hit the ball hard enough so that it will roll only slightly beyond the cup if you miss the putt. "Never up, never in" is still a true statement. Read the green, study the roll or hill for each stroke, and become familiar with the texture of the green. To assure that short putts are stroked straight to the hole, paint a stripe around the ball. Align the stripe with the cup, and if the ball is stroked properly, the stripe will roll over and over in a straight line. If the ball is stroked on an angle, a spin will be imparted to the ball, causing the stripe to wobble as the ball rolls to the cup.

If you develop trouble after having learned the fundamentals from a qualified instructor, do not attempt self-diagnosis; consult a golf professional. The professional knows best how to diagnose and remedy the faults that may feel natural even though they are causing trouble. Many golfers change some part of the swing to compensate for too rapid or too slow rotation of the hips; but as in everything, so in golf, two wrongs seldom make a right.

Practice, if done properly, can be a big asset in furthering the enjoyment of the game; too much practice, however, with accompanying fatigue, may induce bad habits. Know your tolerance and stay within your limits.

SELECTION OF CLUB

There are several factors to consider when selecting the right club to reach the green; the most important is your ability to hit the ball. To determine this ability, practice by selecting a target at a known distance, and note how close the hits land. Continue this practice until you know how far you hit consistently.

The establishment of the range for each club is of little value without the ability to judge distances. A simple method to develop judgment of distance is to compare the area with some well-known distance. A football field, for example, is 100 yards long; thus, when on a golf course, visualize a football field in determining distances you have covered or that remain. Other distances include a city block, the driveway of a house, or some other familiar distance. Since no instrument or gauge may be used to ascertain distance, the ability to judge distance is essential when playing a shot to the green. About 80 percent of golfers tend to underclub themselves, or use a club that is not capable of carrying the

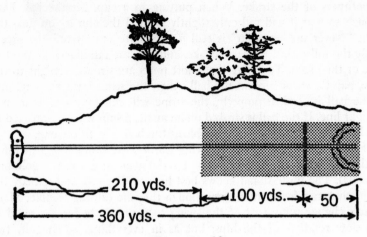

210 yds.   100 yds.   50

360 yds.

Illustration 18

ball the distance required. A good rule of thumb is: it is often better to be long on a shot than to land in front of the green, an area usually well trapped (see Illus. 18).

The wind is important in planning a shot. A side wind may have little effect on distance, but will cause the ball to drift to one side. When hitting into the wind, choose a club at least one number lower than you would ordinarily use to reach the green. The lower flight of the ball makes it less subject to wind resistance. Hitting with the wind will be the opposite, and a higher numbered club is used, since the wind assists the flight of the ball. Also, a ball hit into the wind will have more backspin and will stop in a shorter distance than one hit with the wind. All of this will depend, of course, on how hard the wind is blowing.

The lie of the ball is another factor in selecting a club to be used. Hitting to an elevated green from an uphill lie will require more club (a lower-numbered club) than hitting to a green the same distance away but on the same level or on a level lower than the ball.

GLOSSARY

7

Terms* Related to Golf Clubs

Cap: The plastic disc at the top of the grip.
Face: The hitting surface of the clubhead.
Head: The heavy metal or wood part of the club that strikes the ball.
Heel: The rear part of the clubhead.
Insert: Plastic imbedded in the hitting surface of the head of a wood club.
Neck or hosel: Part of the club where the shaft joins the head.
Plug: The wood piece inserted in the top of the shaft.
Shaft: The handle of the club.
Sole: The bottom of the clubhead. Also, the act of placing the club on the ground at address.
Toe: The tip end of the clubhead.

Terms Related to Strokes

Ace: A hole in one.
Approach: Stroke played to the green.
Birdie: One stroke under par.
Bogey: One stroke over par.
Chip shot: A short shot played to the green.
Divot: Sod cut with the clubhead after it hits the ball.
Eagle: Two strokes under par.
Explode: To take a large quantity of sand when hitting out of a sand trap (bunker).
Fan: A stroke that misses the ball (see *Wiff*).
Fore: A warning call to anyone in the way of an approaching ball.
Forward press: A slight shift of weight to the forward foot to start the backswing.
Half swing: A swing in which the clubhead is brought only halfway back.

* All terms in this Glossary are defined for right-handed players.

Hole out: To sink the ball into the cup.

Hook: A ball hit with a counterclockwise spin, which sends it in a curve to the left of the intended line of flight.

Loft: Angle at which the clubhead is joined to the shaft; also, the trajectory of the ball in the air.

Par: The score an expert is expected to make for any hole.

Pitch: A short lofted shot, with a backspin, to the green.

Pull: To hit the ball in a straight line to the left.

Push: To hit the ball in a straight line to the right.

Putt: To play a stroke on the green with a putter.

Scuff: To scrape or cut the turf with the clubhead before impact with the ball.

Shank: Hitting the ball with the heel and neck of the club, sending it to the right.

Slice: A ball hit with a clockwise spin, which sends it in a curve to the right of the intended line of flight.

Stroke: Forward movement of the club with the intention of striking the ball.

Topped ball: A ball hit across the top, so that it just rolls along the ground.

Waggle: Preliminary wrist flexion, causing the club to swing forward and backward. Often used to relieve tension.

Wiff: Missing the ball entirely (see *Fan*).

Terms Related to Stance

Address: Position assumed by a player in preparation for hitting the ball.

Closed stance: The left foot placed slightly forward of the right, closer to the line of flight.

Open stance: The right foot placed slightly closer than the left to the line of direction.

Square stance: The toes of both feet parallel to the line of direction.

Stance: Position of the feet.

Terms Related to the Golf Course

Apron: The closely cut part of the fairway immediately adjacent to the green.

Bunker: A hazard placed in a fairway; it may be a mound of ground planted with grass, or a sand trap.

Casual water: A temporary accumulation of water, not recognized as a hazard of the course.

Course: The play area, with either nine or eighteen holes.

Cup: The hole sunk into the green into which the ball must be played.

Dog leg: A curve in the fairway to the right or left.

Fairway: The well-kept portion of terrain between the tee and the green.

Flagstick: The marker in the hole on the green.

Green: The closely cut area which contains the cup and the flag.

Hazard: Any bunker or water designated by the rules committee as an area to increase the difficulty of the course.

Lie: The manner in which the ball in play is resting.

Links: The golf course.

Loose impediment: Any obstruction not fixed or growing.

Out-of-bounds: Ground outside the course from which play is prohibited. This area is usually marked with white stakes.

Rough: Heavy, long grass fringing the green or fairway.

Tee: A wooden peg or other material used in starting play from the teeing surface.

Teeing ground: Often referred to as the tee. Starting place for the hole to be played.

Tee markers: Two objects on the teeing area which determine the front and side limits of the teeing ground.

Terms Related to Matches and Tournaments

Fourball play: Two players opposing two other players, each side playing its better ball, or the ball with which the better score was made.

Foursome: A match in which two players play against two, each side playing one ball.

Match: A contest between two or more players or sides.

Match play: Competition in which results are determined by number of holes won.

Medalist: The player who has the lowest qualifying score in a tournament.

Nassau: A type of scoring in a match-play tournament in which one point is allotted for the winner of the first nine; one point for the second nine; and one point for the 18 holes.

Stroke play: Stroke competition in which results are determined by the number of strokes played.

Terms Related to Rules

Away: The ball farthest from the flagstick.

Dormie: A player or a side having won as many more holes from his opponent as there are holes remaining to be played.

Halved: Opponents complete a hole with the same number of strokes.

Handicaps: Strokes granted to equalize playing ability.

Honor: The side or player having priority on a tee. It is decided by lot, by player, or by side winning previous hole.

Penalty stroke: A stroke added to a player's score for infringement of certain rules.

Playing through: Allowing a group of players to pass another group.

Provisional ball: A ball played when the player feels a previous ball has been lost or is out-of-bounds.

Summer Rules: Regular playing rules of golf apply.

Winter Rules or Preferred Lies: Permission is granted, usually on score cards, to improve the lie of the ball on the fairway.

SELF-TESTING
AND EVALUATION

Score Card. The score card contains much valuable information concerning play on a course, especially a strange course. Some of the information included is: length of the hole, men's and women's par; order of strokes to be given when handicap is used; space for scoring stroke or match play, and local ground rules. On many cards a schematic drawing of the course is shown to aid the stranger in determining the direction to follow.

Distance. The distance of the hole, measured from the center of the teeing ground through the middle of the fairway to the center of the green, is shown in yards. This information is important in determining the choice of club for each shot. If a ball is driven approximately 220 yards and the card shows the distance of the hole to be 390 yards, a quick calculation will reveal that 170 yards remain. This can be an accurate basis for proper club selection. Because of the variation in terrain, a player may often be deceived in his judgment of distance; this deception, however, may be eliminated by referral to distances listed on the score card.

Par. Par is computed on distances an expert is capable of hitting the ball, and allows for two putts on each green. The following yardages are usually the basis for determining par for a hole:

Men	*Women*
Up to 250 yards—3 strokes	Up to 210 yards—3 strokes
251 — 470 yards—4 strokes	211 — 400 yards—4 strokes
471 — up　　—5 strokes	401 — 575 yards—5 strokes
	576 — up　　　—6 strokes

These distances are not arbitrary in the determining of par, because consideration must be given to the relative difficulty of each hole. For example, a hole 400 yards in length may be a par five because of the number and placement of hazards, or the presence of a deep ravine leading to a narrow fairway. Following are terms used to describe scores under or over par:

> *Double Eagle:* Three strokes under par
> *Eagle:* Two strokes under par
> *Birdie:* One stroke under par
> *Bogey:* One stroke over par
> *Double Bogey:* Two strokes over par
> *Triple Bogey:* Three strokes over par

Handicap. The number listed under handicap strokes shows the order in which strokes are given in a match of differing handicaps. This order is based on the difficulty of the holes; if only one stroke is to be given, it will be given on the hole listed as number one in the handicap strokes column. If the handicap difference between the two players is six strokes, these strokes are given on holes listed as one through six in the handicap strokes column. The above refers to match play only. In stroke play, the total handicap is subtracted from the total score, resulting in the net score.

Score. In many tournaments, score is kept by the player for his opponent, or by scorekeepers. In match play, a hole won is designated by a plus (+) in the column provided; a hole lost is marked by a minus (−). A hole tied or halved is designated by a zero (0) (see Illustration 19). During the match, players check with their scorers on the accuracy of the score and the status of the match. In match play the game is over when a player has won more holes than are left to be played. If a player has won three more holes than his opponent, and there are only two holes left to play, the match ends in a score of 3 and 2. The two remaining holes are not played, and do not count in the match. In stroke play all holes are played and the number of strokes determines the winner.

Ground rules. Most courses have local ground rules, or interpretations of various hazards. These rules are to be followed as well as the United States Golf Association rules. Ground under repair, boundary markers, and drainage ditches are usually explained on the card. These should be studied carefully before playing on a strange course.

Hole		1	2	3	4	5	6	7	8	9	out
Yards		343	369	195	348	378	202	413	515	375	3138
Men's Par		4	4	3	4	4	3	4	5	4	35
Self	*Jack*	5	4	3							
Part	*Ann*	6	7	6							
We	|+ − 0	0	+	−							
Handicap Strokes		11	8	16	12	6	14	5	1	7	
They	|+ − 0	0	−	+							
Oppt	*Joe*	5	6	4							
Oppt	*Mary*	6	6	4							
Women's Par		4	4	3	4	4	3	5	5	4	36

Illustration 19

Handicaps

To enable the average or poor player to compete successfully with the expert, the United States Golf Association has developed a system for computing handicaps, based upon current scores made on courses with different degrees of difficulty. This system, put into effect January 1, 1967, assigns a single handicap to each player. This handicap is based not only on scores received, but also on the difficulty of the course or courses on which the player has made these scores.

Formerly a committee of qualified experts determined the rating of the course based on the average number of strokes taken by an expert playing the course ten times. Under the new regulation the course is rated primarily by yardage. Any adjustment from the yardage rating is made for the over-all course and not for any one hole. Such things as water hazards, bunkers, and size of greens can be considered in the over-all rating.

Present handicaps are computed on the handicap differentials of the player's lowest ten scores from his last twenty rounds. The handicap differential is the difference between the player's score and the course rating. For example, if the player scores an 82 and the course rating is 70, the handicap differential will be 12. Eighty-five percent of the total of the lowest ten handicap differentials for a player will be his handicap.

If the player's ten lowest scores average 90 on a course with a rated difficulty of 70, the average handicap differential would be 20. His handicap would be 17, 85 percent of 20.

Estimated scores are allowed on holes not completed. If a player has a handicap of 18 or less he may pick up on as many as four holes, and record a double bogey. Should his handicap be 19 or more he may pick up on as many as five holes and record a triple bogey. This will tend to speed up match play competition where one player has obviously lost the hole and can pick up without loss of his score being counted toward his handicap. The maximum handicap for both men and women is 36.

The handicap system enables an average player to compete with the expert on an equal basis. A player whose handicap is eight will receive six strokes from a player whose handicap is two. These strokes are to be given on the holes in the order assigned on the score card.

Some districts or courses have systems that vary slightly from that of the United States Golf Association. Professionals of the various courses will have the necessary information to determine handicaps. Many courses have tournaments based upon one-day handicaps. Lack of space prohibits a thorough discussion of these systems, but each golfer should be aware that varied methods of computing handicaps do exist.

SELF-ANALYSIS SCORE CARD

The score card may be used to help analyze your game. When playing alone, or with others, you can tabulate your own score on your individual card in the manner explained. When playing with others, the score for the group should be kept on another score card.

On your score card, label the sections as follows:

Self: Drive R/L yds.—distance of drive, and whether drive is to right or left of fairway.

Part.: Iron or wood R/L yds.—distance of 2, 3, 4, or 5 irons or woods, and direction.

Opp.: Pitch R/L yds. (from cup)—distance from cup with 6, 7, 8, or 9 irons, and direction.

Opp.: Chip R/L yds. (from cup)—distance from cup of chip shot, and direction.

Putt yds. from cup—distance from cup.

Putt total—total number of putts.

Thus your personal score card should look like this:

Hole		1	2	3	4	5	6	7	8	9	out
Yards											
Men's Par											
Self	*Drive* *R-L-yds*										
Part	*Iron or wood* *R-L-yds*										
We	*Putt-yds-cup*										
Handicap strokes											
They	*Putt total*										
Oppt	*Pitch* *R-L-yds*										
Oppt	*Chip* *R-L-yds*										
Women's Par											

Score card converted to self-analysis card
Illustration 20

The number of items included will depend upon the size of the card and the spaces available. Make as many entries in one block as needed. For example, if more than one long iron shot is hit on one hole, record them all in the one block.

As soon as you have driven, record the approximate driving distance and direction in the appropriate block. Follow the same procedure with the long iron, the pitch, and chip shots. When on the green, record how far from the cup the first putt landed, and the total number of putts taken. If desired, the total strokes for the hole may be recorded in the margin of the score card.

Using the score card in this manner will enable you to make an analysis of your total game; the length and direction of drives and long iron shots; the frequency of a slice or hook; the distance from the cup and accuracy of pitch and chip shots; the distance from the cup of the first putt; and the total number of putts needed. Keeping this kind of record each time you play will give you a basis for comparison and improvement.

GOLF ANALYSIS CHART

Stance
  Weight balanced
  Knees relaxed
  Feet positioned   _____

Grip
  V's of both hands
  Two knuckles visible
  Thumb positions   _____
  Finger grip
  Right palm over left thumb
  Firm—not tight

Posture and swing

Backswing
  Waggle or forward press
  Clubhead along ground
  Left arm straight
  Head steady   _____
  Base stable
  Proper rotation
  Right leg straight
  Club parallel at top

Contact
  Uncoil
  Weight distribution
  Eyes focused on ball   _____
  Wrists firm
  Force exerted down and through
  Solid hit

Follow through
  Clubhead follows ball
  Right shoulder lifts head
  Proper rotation   _____
  Left leg straight
  Firm left side

Total Swing

| Relaxed | ☐ | Synchronized | ☐ | Rhythmical | ☐ | Smooth | ☐ |
| Tense | ☐ | Choppy | ☐ | Unbalanced | ☐ | Jerky | ☐ |

Comments:

NOTE: It would be impossible for an observer to notice all the above items during one swing; however, these items are intended to aid in focusing the attention of the observer on specific parts of the swing during repeated observations. An appraisal of the total swing can be given by checking as many items as necessary.

GOLF ANALYSIS CHART

The chart on page 52 may be used to analyze the golf swing after you understand the fundamentals. You may use this chart as a check list for your own swing, partners may use it to analyze each other's swing, or one person may analyze swings of several others.

The items listed are self-explanatory, and need only be checked if the golfer needs more work on any of them. Practice on the items checked should improve the game.

QUESTIONS FOR STUDY

These questions are listed not only to check knowledge of the various facets of the game but to stimulate some thought about the game. They are not all-inclusive, nor are they intended to give any particular emphasis, but are presented as a guide.

1. What factors govern the proper club selection for a specific shot?
2. How is a ball hit to produce backspin?
3. How is distance judged on a chip shot?
4. Why is balance important in golf?
5. List six suggestions to follow when hitting the ball from a sand trap; when putting.
6. How is the honor determined at each hole?
7. List some causes of a slice; of a hook.
8. Define: bogey, eagle, birdie, double bogey.
9. What is meant by the term "par"?
10. What is meant by the expression, "Drive for show and putt for dough"?
11. Why is it important to carry a score card even though you are not the scorekeeper?
12. How can one be assured of getting a set of clubs to fit his particular build and swing?
13. What is the penalty for grounding the club in a hazard?
14. What is the difference between stroke and match play?
15. Explain the differences between woods and irons.

16. What are some points of etiquette to be observed on the green?

17. How has the establishment of a handicap system contributed to the popularity of the game?

18. Why is a change in the grip advocated for putting?

19. What is the USGA? The PGA?

20. Why is the backswing such an important part of the swing?

21. Will players with the same handicap, although established on courses of different difficulty, play even?

22. What is meant by "needing a firm left wrist"?

23. What are the basic differences in the various grips?

24. Why is the position of the hands so important in the swing?

25. From whom may you seek and receive advice while playing?

26. What procedure would you follow to be able to tee off on number 1?

27. How and where would you, as a member of a foursome, tally your own score for each hole?

28. Why is it important to know the kind and number of the golf ball you are using?

29. How far may a ball be moved from a fixed obstruction?

30. Whose responsibility is it to smooth out the sand in a hazard after a shot has been made?

31. Who determines when a ball is unplayable?

32. Why are instruments or devices for measuring distances considered illegal?

33. Are there any rules governing the selection of club to be used anywhere on the course?

34. What is the penalty for playing a ball belonging to someone else?

35. What is meant by "winter rules"?

36. When do you "mark" a ball on the green?

37. How do you determine the direction to hit a ball on the green?

38. Describe the stance used when hitting a ball from a position on the fairway, sloping up to the green.

39. List five items found on a score card.

40. Why are the higher-numbered irons used on a pitch shot?

41. Where is the best place to stand when your partner is hitting the ball?

42. When is it wise to have the flagstick removed from the cup?

43. Explain the statement, "In golf, rhythm is more important than power."

44. How is the consistency of the sand in a bunker determined?

45. What is the approximate distance for the width of the stance on the drive?

46. Why is a chip shot called a "hit and run"?

47. Why is a steady head position so important in golf?

48. Why do many professionals advise a waggle and forward press?

49. Explain what is meant by "the social values of golf."

50. Describe the relationship between the path of the clubhead and the flight of the ball.

BIBLIOGRAPHY 9

Armour, Tommy. *How to Play Your Best Golf* (New York: Simon and Schuster, 1953).
(Paperback, 1964.) A simple and direct approach to the fundamentals of golf. The instructions and illustrations are easy to follow for the beginner and the low-handicap player.

Armour, Tommy. *A Round of Golf with Tommy Armour* (New York: Simon and Schuster, 1959).
The book is just what the title implies. Mr. Armour assists you in playing a round of golf. He explains how different shots should be made and cautions you about the many pitfalls confronting the average golfer.

Boros, Julius. *How to Play Par Golf* (Englewood Cliffs, N.J.: Prentice-Hall, 1953).
The author stresses knowledge of fundamentals and development of a consistent swing pattern. His explanations of the basics are excellent.

Casper, Billy. *Golf Shotmaking* (Garden City, N.Y.: Doubleday & Co., 1966).
Explanations of various shots made during a round are given by the author. He starts with the fading tee shot and takes you through the lag putt. Examples of the needs for the various shots are made by the author as he relates his tournament experiences. The more advanced player would benefit from this book.

Cranford, Peter G. *The Winning Touch in Golf* (New York: Brumhall House, 1961).
The author, a psychologist, uses his experiences and observations to give a better understanding of the why's of the game. There are excellent practice and training suggestions throughout the book.

Dante, J., and L. Diegal. *The Nine Bad Shots in Golf* (New York: McGraw-Hill Book Co., 1947).
The nine bad shots usually encountered by the golfer are explained with suggestions for corrections. The instructions are clear and easy to follow.

Dey, Joseph C. Jr. *Golf Rules in Pictures* (New York: Grosset & Dunlap, revised annually).
A publication of the United States Golf Association, this book which explains and interprets the rules and etiquette of the game, is the best available reference to the rules. The illustrations are excellent in presenting the problems under discussion.

East, J. Victor. *Better Golf in Five Minutes* (Englewood Cliffs, N.J.: Prentice-Hall, 1956).
A clear and concise practice pattern is explained in this book. The author explains how, through consistent and intelligent practice, the beginner can play well.

Ford, Doug. *The Wedge Book* (South Norwalk, Conn.: Golf Digest, 1963).
The various uses of the wedge are explained. The author stresses the importance of this club and its proper uses. The instruction is well written and the illustrations are excellent.

Hogan, Ben. "The Modern Fundamentals of Golf" *Sports Illustrated.* Vol. VI, Nos. 10–14, March-April, 1957.
A series of articles in which the author makes a scholarly analysis of the golf swing. Particular attention is paid to minute details. An excellent resource for the person with an understanding of the mechanical and muscular bases of the golf swing.

Hogan, Ben. *Hogan's Five Lessons on the Modern Fundamentals* (New York: A. S. Barnes & Co., 1957).
The instructional material in the book is adapted from the series published in *Sports Illustrated*. The material is detailed particularly on the analysis of the golf swing. The illustrations are exceptionally well done.

Jones, Robert Tyre. *Bobby Jones On Golf* (Garden City, N.Y.: Doubleday & Co., 1966).
This book is an expansion of a series of golf instruction articles and related experiences of the author during his playing career. The material is excellent reading as well as informative. The many hints and suggestions given by the author are indispensable to the serious player.

Middlecoff, Cary. *Master Guide to Golf* (Englewood Cliffs, N.J.: Prentice-Hall, 1960).
The problems of golf from A to W, addressing the ball to wind shots, are discussed. Instruction and suggestions for improvement are well done. The book is well organized for a ready reference to all phases of the game.

National Golf Foundation, *Golf Lessons* (Chicago: National Golf Foundation, 1965).
A teaching manual for the beginner. The authors are experts at teaching and have organized the material so the beginner can easily follow the instruction. All phases of the game are covered.

Player, Gary. *Gary Player's Golf Secrets* (Englewood Cliffs, N.J.: Prentice-Hall, 1962).
The author relates his experiences with various parts of the game. The hints and suggestions are summarized at the end of each chapter, after a discussion of the shot. The mental side of golf is given a place of importance in the book.

Price, Charles (Editor). *Golf Magazine's Pro-Pointers & Stroke Savers* (New York: Harper & Bros., 1960).
A collection of various hints and suggestions from various pros on all parts of the game. An excellent reference.

Rees, Dia. *The Key to Golf* (New York: A. S. Barnes & Co., 1961).
The author, a British golf champion, presents his ideas in four segments, i.e., How to Play, Common Faults, Odds and Ends, Questions, and Glossary. The instruction is basic and understandable. Suggestions for curing common faults are thorough and easy to follow. A discussion of golf etiquette and rules is timely for the beginner.

Rosbury, Bob. *The Putter Book* (South Norwalk, Conn.: Golf Digest, 1963).
A thorough and complete discussion of all phases of putting is made. The author gives hints and suggestions of everything from the putting grip to reading the greens. Selection of a putter, an often overlooked problem, is discussed thoroughly.

Snead, Sam. *The Driver Book* (South Norwalk, Conn.: Golf Digest, 1963).
Sam Snead, reputed as having the "picture" swing explains the importance of hitting a good drive, then explains how it is done. The instruction is easy to follow. Words of caution about developing faults with the driver are included.

Wind, Herbert Warren. *Tips from the Top* (Englewood Cliffs, N.J.: Prentice-Hall, 1955).
A compilation of tips given by the top teaching and playing pros in the country. An excellent reference.

MAGAZINES

"Golf," Published monthly by Universal Publishing and Distributing Corporation, 234 East 45th St., New York, N.Y. Subscriptions taken at Box 513, Des Moines, Iowa 50302

"Golf Digest," Published monthly by Golf Digest, Inc., 88 Scribner Ave., Norwalk, Conn. 06856

"Golf World," Published weekly. Box 2000, Southern Pines, N.C. 28387